GIFT SONGS

John Burnside

CAPE POETRY

Published by Jonathan Cape 2007

2 4 6 8 10 9 7 5 3 1

Copyright © John Burnside 2007

First published in Great Britain in 2007 by
Jonathan Cape
Random House, 20 Vauxhall Bridge Road,
London SW1V 2SA

www.randomhouse.co.uk

Addresses for companies within The Random House Group Limited
can be found at: www.randomhouse.co.uk

The Random House Group Limited Reg. No. 954009

A CIP catalogue record for this book is
available from the British Library

ISBN 0224 07997 2

The Random House Group Limited makes every effort to ensure that the papers
used in its books are made from trees that have been legally sourced from well-
managed and credibly certified forests. Our paper procurement policy can be
found at: www.randomhouse.co.uk/paper.htm

Typeset in Bembo by Palimpsest Book Production Limited, Grangemouth, Stirlingshire
Printed and bound in Great Britain by William Clowes Ltd, Beccles, Suffolk

for Lucas and Gil

And Jacob asked him, and said, Tell me, I pray thee, thy name.
And he said, Wherefore is it that thou dost ask after my name?
And he blessed him there.

Genesis, xxxii, 29

Fiction's inside like faith.
It doesn't count unless you believe it, and
you don't have to know it for it to be the truth.

Rodney Jones

CONTENTS

RESPONSES TO AUGUSTINE OF HIPPO

GIFT SONGS

FOUR QUARTETS

RESPONSES TO AUGUSTINE OF HIPPO

I DE CORPORIS RESURRECTIONE

for George Soule

The snowdrops are here;

and sometimes the dead we have washed
and buried:

the sweet-mouthed, arthritic mothers we rarely noticed
polishing spoons in the small hours
                                        polishing mirrors;

the men in our kitchens blurring with silicosis;
                                        the gradual dead
drifting between the trees like gusts of wind

and finding a visible form
                        an approximate colour:
aconite; meltwater; cinnabar; Prussian blue;

the dead we have named and buried
                                        breaking like waves
on sandstone and leaf
                        on tree-bark and rusted iron.

The snowdrops are an exercise in white:
not quite convincing
                        flowers that would have been green
in a world without shadows;

but only the dead are green
in the last days of winter;

only the dead we have numbered and set aside
will blossom again in ditch-moss and columns of ivy

replacing themselves in the lull of the visible world
with fingerprints; voices, blood blisters; rose tattoos.

———————————

Like turning aside and living a season or two
in another room:

snow at the window for days
and the heat in your fingers

leaching away through the glass
like remembered skin.

Or how you would turn for a moment
from what you were doing

to notice the dark
at three in the afternoon

and how the earth calls out for every death,
contriving apples, mole-runs, tiny birds

alive inside the gold japonica
and waiting for the moment to arrive

when song begins; the black
transformed to green.

———————————

I thought he would come at dawn:
dark feet crossing the yard or a lukewarm
shadow in the angle of the wall,

dew trails and traces of frost in a downstairs
cupboard, or an afterthought of myrrh
fading to mist in the mist of the bathroom mirror;

and, even now, when everything is cause
for doubt, I still imagine a return,
though never quite the god they talked about

in Sunday school: more atmosphere than flesh,
this almost taking form as frequency,
like static, or the fuzz of radio

that might have been the voice in everything:
a music I was promised in the sleep
of childhood, when the first snow reached the edge

of waiting and the constancy of this
– the still to come, the gracile revelation –
hovered between the looked-for and the given.

———————————

We weren't prepared for this:
                                        a shimmer of eyes
and the shore road blurring with sand
in the evening wind;

just as we're never prepared
for the soul, when it happens:
the owl face stitched to the dark; the sudden burn;

or how a stairwell fills, some cloudless night,
with something like a held breath, or a voice
about to speak.

Only an hour after midnight
the cold tastes of cherries:

a slow thread of light in the stairwell
                        the still of the basement
patient and dark as the phantoms we carry away
from an edited life.

Out on the porch the wind chimes sing for themselves
but the sky is another room
in this dream of a house:

the sycamores framing the yard like a detail from Breughel,
the line between wintering bark and the limelight of snow
the shift in a long conversation
                        or one of those games

where the nothing that happens in time
is the one thing we have

for keeps:
            the seep of music through the bone;
a wavelength of owls, where everything is static.

II   AMA ET FAC QUOD VIS

for Piritta Maavuori

The God of Saint Paul, who is
'no respecter of persons'

might just as easily have been
the self

      – that loves what it will
and watches us quicken and fade
with the passing of time

as calmly as we watch our shadows form
and lengthen, with each shift and slant of light.

        Silence is argument carried on by other means
                    Ernesto Guevara

What we intend
and what we allow to happen

is anyone's guess.

All week my voice was failing – first husky, then strained,
till it guttered away to a whisper

and disappeared;
            guttered away

this morning, when the snow began to fall,
whiting out streets and gardens, muffling the cars,

7

until it seemed the only good reply
was silence:
                    not

the quiet of dismay,
but what Guevara thought of as the argument
continued – *carried on*

by other means – that cold and salty pact
the body makes with things unlike itself

– a snowfall, or a gust of Russian wind,
the evanescence of an upper room
that might be something new, or someone gone

a moment since:
                    and how it is transformed
by what it never finds:
                    no soul; no

shadow.

———————

Propose what you like;
                    propose
causality
        the notion of the self
how one thing follows another
in grim succession

it only takes a moment in the wind
to break that argument.

Consider the body: changeable, incomplete,
yet still continuous:
think how it holds the perfect likenesses
of all the former selves that it is not,
how casually it gathers and renews
the forms we have scarcely noticed – winter buds,

a flock of starlings turning on the air,
the bleached grass skirting the lake
                                    or the snake-bark of maples –

and how, on a morning like this, with our everyday lives
suspended
              in these white parentheses

we start again from scratch: the coming night;
the ferry that runs to the island;
                                    the sullen ice;

the shapes we have scarcely noticed, bearing us on
to all we have yet to become
                        to the blank of a future.

———————————

I wake in the dark and the dream evaporates before I can grasp
the details

– something about a bell, and prints in the snow;
my dream self distinct from the person I seem in waking;

my dream self, bright and light-footed,
a holy, unclouded soul, tracking these prints
to the edge of a sycamore wood –

the details blurring and suddenly melting away
and only a moment's afterlife of joy:
the body a solid again, the mind a distraction,
the net of the slipshod entangling the peregrine heart.

———————————

In the small hours
awake and alone,

waiting for snow, or watching the snow as it falls,
from an upper room,

as far as I am from home,
and as strange as I seem,

what could I really prefer
to the weight of the self?

its deftness, on nights like this,
its immutable grace,

the only means I have
of bearing witness.

———————————

This morning I followed a trail
to the edge of the woods,

then felt the shadow watching as I lost
my nerve:
          a brightness

slipped behind the rain;
an aftermath
                of lanolin and dust.

———————————

Now I look back from the warmth
of a scentless house

with something foreign
cradled in my chest

and wonder that I took its weight
for safety, all those nights I passed untouched

and dreaming,
like a calf lulled in the dark

while something sweet
unfolds along the blade,

lifeblood
            or rapture
taken for a song.

III DE LIBERO ARBITRIO

for Johanna Lane

– something that comes
from the dark
(not
self or not-self)

but something between the two
like the shimmering line
where one form defines another
yet fails to end;

look for the proof in snow
or the bleed of light
between the shorefront
and the harbour wall

this late December evening:
nothing there;
but listen, and it sounds
like wings arriving
quietly over the firth

and further out
the snow
is also falling

as surely as it falls upon the lawns
and hedges
in this narrow seaside town.

I wonder how we know the things we know
most surely
        with no hope of evidence
and lacking a faith
        that might extend to heaven

stopping from time to time,
        on nights like this,
to see it all again
        – the sky, the firth,

the empty street
        where someone walks ahead
and leaves a trail of footprints
        through the darkness –

_____

Not that we ever return
        but the people we were
remain in that snowlit room
        with the distance between them.

The light on a cotton blouse
        the scent of the garden
perhaps it has rained in the night
        or a moment since

the absolute white of a sleeve
        and a blackbird singing
somewhere among the shrubs
        still wet with rain

or only the smell of coffee
        whatever there was
persists
        so it seems they are waiting

the people we were
        who said
or omitted to say
        the appropriate words

waiting for something to end
        though it hasn't begun
waiting for us to go back
        with what we know now

to rescue them
        one detail at a time:
a coffee cup, a bird,
        the smell of rain

the word unspoken
        silently deleted.

The shapes we mistake
for love
        – a garden in summer;
that sound the wind makes
pausing in the leaves;

the shapes we mistake
for ourselves

at the edge of the water
          – turning a moment
then slipping away to a depth
that never existed

that hint
          of *jadis et naguère*
while the moment lasted

and always the sound
          of a future we could have refused:
a household of card-games and desk-lamps,
          a bed of carnations

the promise we made
          even then
to continue alone.

IV   RETRACTATIONES

If, as he says,
the flaw in the weft of the soul

is how it tends, forever,
towards nothingness,

then might we not imagine it
as grace itself,

the way it teeters,
this side of extinction,

locked with a flesh
that is possibly not, after all,

as loathsome as he thought,
but just as much

illumined, steady,
pitched just at the point

where everything might stop,
and nothing happens;

———————————

and how it resembles love is the way
it might be the last occasion, sitting alone
in the kitchen, as dusk filters in;

how any moment now, the known might end,
or end for me, at least, while, somewhere else,
someone is cooking a meal, or writing a letter.

Out in the garden, the shadows merge with the dark,
till all I have taken for granted – the half-truths of form,
the goodwill of definition –

is folded up, as matter always is,
falling away, like the undelivered soul,
toward nothingness.

As a child, I imagined the silence of the dead
was the silence of disapproval;
or else, a mild distaste for how I went on

living, not quite sure of shapes and colours.
Later, it seemed they had stumbled upon a world
so innocent of names, the whole event

was one enormous household, beasts and angels
simmering like rain against the skin,
as if the soul were not the uttered word,

as if the colours were those perfect forms
he always wanted: blithe, Platonic blues
and reds, and not the accidents of light

that shift and flicker in the fading lawn,
the dimming fire amidst the Deutzia,
antirrhinums, milkweed, evening primrose.

Yet surely the dead are soulless, not being here,
where souls are made
in shadows and greening leaves:

soulless, and poised at the rim
of chaos, they long to return,
to sit up alone all night, in kitchens like this,

remembering,
forgetting,
being lost.

As a child I imagined the life beyond this life
as one enormous room, all
mist and kinship,

now I would have to insist on walls and factions,
hidden compartments, corridors leading off
to secret gardens steeped in changing light,

not to be set apart, but to meet again
in the old way, coming together
by chance, on an aimless walk

through foxgloves, or Michaelmas daisies,
losing and winning back
the sense of the other,

sun on a stranger's skin, and that quickening
when someone else is there,
as yet unseen:

———————————

and it isn't a choice I would make,
to rise again,

but somewhere between
this one life and the next

I imagine a point
where the soul

is purified:
fogged water leaching through spawn

and the veins
of cowslips;

and this just another event
like an egg, or a sunrise,

a sense of someone waking in the dark
and dressing by a window, looking out

at stars, from time to time, a neighbour's tree,
a sound in the distance like love, or a passing train,

as he teases a bone into place
or straightens a nerve,

preparing to happen again,
in a knowable world,

and all the while puzzled
by something he ought to remember.

GIFT SONGS

VARIETIES OF RELIGIOUS EXPERIENCE

I   SABBATHDAY

The christchild is no distraction
            – the lotus blossom –
seed-pearls of tallow and ice
on the risen body.

Dark by mid-afternoon
when the snow closes in,
sifting us out
from this straggle of lamps and voices,

silence in what we remember,
silence in passing,
silence
in the closing of a door

as something more than light
slips through the gate
and follows the garden wall
past the anxious collie,

all we have left unimagined,
all that is forfeit,
quicksilver, empty as hunger
and never quite seen

when it enters
this cradle of fire
through a gap
in the scriptures

    – the moment when we recognise ourselves
alone, with the blue of medlar, the gold of quince,
and those muslin bags in the half-light, white
as a deposition;

bletting the fruits in the shed
through the year's caesura,
bruise-black and coarse to the touch
while we work and dream,

and all in pursuit
of an essence:
a bittersweet-amber
distillate, not of summer, but of one

decisive morning
– *dew-water; leaf-turn; chill* –
fox-runs threading the lawn
with the promise of dying

but, further away, in the beet-fields,
the unforsaken:
folds in the green of the plural,
unworked, and beginning again.

We were born in the faultlines of paper:
gunpowder, petals of skin, and the white of the eye
dividing, like the flaw in expectation.

Forgive us this day, we said,
in our garment of ashes,
forgive us what is spilt, or not yet come

to pass: *Oh, my
America, my new found land,*

hoarse with the promise of song
and the grace notes of terror.

Time to go back and read it all again,
whiting out the words you understand
till nothing else is visible but this:

shamefaced; gospel; prudent; inexact;
patrimony; silence; coup d'état.

Time to refuse your fifteen minutes of fame,
the prize you've already won, but can never accept,
the small-print on the deed, the no-claims bonus.

Out in the dark, in the cold, in a glimmer of snow,
something you never expected returns to bear witness:
a shadow; a phantom; your double; or something else

that looks like you, or would, if you were there,
come to unravel the ghost of a burnt-out fire,
and raking through clinker and ash, to recover a heartbeat.

It feels like a door in the light
through which the mind might pass at any moment,

arriving like an actor at a scene
you've long rehearsed:

a little market town, perhaps,
with rounds of cheese

and pigeons hung from twine
around the stalls;

a narrow alleyway that looks
familiar, on this rainy afternoon,

the glitter of the lights, the smell of bread,
the windows, with their naked mannequins

contorted and rapt,
like Gray's anatomical drawings;

and, sometimes,
with a little luck or charm,

that inlet on the far side
of the island, where we swam

alone, among the fishes,
in a sea

so clear
we could imagine ourselves healed

and true again
to what we used to know:

the open sky,
the part-song of cicadas.

Only a moth at the glass,
or so it seems,
the animals further away
and indistinct,

wolverine
hitched to your skin
and the dreamed
coyote.

All night they ran in the woods,
till they came to this line
of fence-wire
and poisoned gravel,

desert
behind them,
prairie grass
burning for miles,

salt-flats
and rivers,
birch woods,
an ocean of stars,

but nothing there
to match
this baffled
sleep,

first light gilding the door
like a wayward angel,
day-lilies silvered with rain
in our picturesque yard.

29

Craneflies for millions of years,
unchanged, like a template;

gold matter folded in resin:
katydid   silkworm

yet even under glass
we just make out

the fingerprint,
the single flake of skin,

a dusting of fugitive cells
or a hint of civet;

ten thousand miles
of heroin and myrrh.

Whatever I hoped to believe,
I never imagined
the pitfall of consolation:

weak tea catching the light
in a presbytery kitchen,

the rest of my life – recovery,
restitution –

that room at the end of the hall
where they stored the vestments;

though surely it crossed my mind
on those autumn nights,

given the aubergine pall
on the turn of the stairs,

surely I saw, as only a child can see
the pleasure of making amends
in the lull of the evening,

telling my sins to a shadow,
reciting the penance,

rinsing my soul in His tears
before sinning again.

The mice are back;
                I leave them
crusts and pine-nuts
                on the kitchen
counter,
        leave them
treats they sometimes
        miss,
                experiments
with milk and berries,
spelt
        and pumpkin seeds.
I like it
        that I have
                such neighbours
– not
        invisible
                but moving back and forth
between their world
                and mine
discreetly;
        I enjoy
their table manners
        when I catch a glimpse
of something reddish-grey
        that I have
interrupted
        darting for the wall
though not from dread so much
as care
        – an animal
propriety –

   and what they leave behind
as guesswork,
   what this vanishing suggests
is how a man might
   prosper
     if he dared
making himself at home
   without a sound,
adept
   unledgered
     loyal to his burden.

When we are gone
our lives will continue without us

– or so we believe and,
at times, we have tried to imagine

the gaps we will leave being filled
with the brilliance of others:

someone else gathering plums
from this tree in the garden,

someone else thinking this thought
in a room filled with stars

and coming to no conclusion
other than this –

this bungled joy, this inarticulate
conviction that the future cannot come

without the grace
of setting things aside,

of giving up
the phantom of a soul

that only seemed to be
while it was passing.

All afternoon I have heard you
going from room to room, as if you would offer
the gift of a watchful presence, the gift of a look
to how the sunlight gathers in the folds
of curtains
            how the shadows on the wall
flit back and forth, more sparrow, or swallow in flight
than birds would have been.

Like you I have felt it today, that space in our house
where doors might swing open
                          messengers appear:
the curve of a bowl, or the red in a vase of carnations
softly assuming the forms of a visitation.

We go for weeks and never catch ourselves
like this, the trace of magic we possess
locked in the work of appearing, day after day,
in the world of our making;

we go for months with phantoms in our heads
till, filling a bath, or fetching the laundry in,
we see ourselves again, at home, illumined,
folding a sheet, or pouring a glass of milk,
bright in the here and now, and unencumbered.

FIVE ANIMALS

It was luck, I suppose,
though it felt like something else
when I pulled off the road
and stopped in a covert of snow
to stretch my legs

and the Arctic fox
came silently out of the distance,
half-way to summer already, the silvery fur
threaded with auburn
and brown, the face

indifferent, although it caught my eye
and watched, for a minute
– scenting me,
sounding me out –
though only, I thought,

from politeness, and not
surprise,
accustomed,
as I was not,
to the rule of the tundra,

the logic of the wilderness that says
where nothing seems to happen
all the time
what happens is the chance
that something might.

When they sing from the harbour wall, amongst
the soured lines and ten-fathom creels,
it sounds like an apprenticeship for something more
auspicious
            – fulmar, say,
for whom this salt-sweet air is neither
fate, nor home;

or half a mile inland, far in the shade
beneath a wind-glazed kirk, the mistle thrush
recalls itself, like something from a dream,
and closes softly on a purer song;

but why would they dream of rebirth, who are
intent on nothing, flitting back and forth
along the shore-front, in a tide of stones?
Everything feeds them: hairweed, shadows, light,

and every crevice is another house
of spice and water, echo to that twin
who wanders in the mountains, almost smoke
between the river and a sky of bone.

For days I come and go
in a dream of feathers,

my fingers a flurry of light
as I fill the kettle,

my house the unsettled reflection
of what I have made

from off-cuts and leftover shingle
to house the birds.

At night, my wife lies down
among the saints,

while I sit late
and listen for a sound

beyond the wind,
beyond the creak of wings,

and as I wait, I know,
as blind men know

the distances
in long-familiar rooms,

how little she would care,
or understand,

if something more than warmth
returned with me

on such a night as this,
late in the year

– a rumour of flight,
a gift from the legible world –

lining the bed she has made
with a love beyond measure.

Sunshine at Spalefields crossing;
small rain at Beley bridge;
gilthead hanging from the silvered dark
in the tanks of the fisheries lab.

Three men are cutting the hay
on the road to Kinaldy,
the scent of it filling the car
as I drive to work,

a tractor blocking the lane
and the post van waiting,
the dog from the cottages
havering back and forth
while the pheasants scatter.

Sometimes I think he knows
what nothing can know,
some future state of luck or bitterness
that lends a purpose to this sudden frenzy,

and I guess, for a while,
his whole world smells of miasma,
the intricate sweetness of oil,
the declensions of rain,

a pocket of mildew and hair
in the mole drain, flushed from its cover,
the animal that dips beneath the sickle,
wed to the map of the grass
and unable to run.

It takes imagination not to wish
for something, when the darkness fills with voices;

but why, when they call, do I want to hurry outside,
leaving the door wide open, the lamp still lit,
the radio lulled to sleep
in an empty room?

The chill fills my shirtsleeves, the fingerless, desert chill
of one enormous nightfall on the skin,

and still I hurry on, towards some
epicentre, where the angel waits,
real or implied, to make its annunciation.

Nothing can disappoint me, light begins
and ends, I hurry on,
the desert flickers out, then comes again

elsewhere
           − a gust of wind; a thread of green −
and I keep walking, while the kettle boils,
or something founders by remote control,

the voices calling from the present tense,
restoring me to where the mind leaves off,
the nothing of the self,
                         the here and now.

FOR A FREE CHURCH

I   THE BODY AS METAPHOR

We only imagine it ends
like childhood, or rain:
fever, the purl in the bone, the amended
lustre of the self, all shell and glitter,

as if it had long been decided
that flesh is a journey,
something immense in the blood,
like a summer of locusts,

or something not quite visible, but quick
as birchseed, or the threading of a wire
through sleep and rapture, gathering the hand
that reaches from the light, to close, or open.

No one invents an absence:
cadmium yellow, duckweed, the capercaillie
– see how the hand we would name restrains itself
till all our stories end in monochrome;

the path through the meadow
reaching no logical end;
nothing but colour: bedstraw and ladies' mantle;
nothing sequential; nothing as chapter and verse.

No one invents the quiet that runs in the grass,
the summer wind, the sky, the meadowlark;
and always the gift of the world, the undecided:
first light and damson blue *ad infinitum*.

Give me a little less
with every dawn:
colour, a breath of wind,
the perfection of shadows,

till what I find, I find
because it's there,
gold in the seams of my hands
and the night light, burning.

Last day of harbour;
rain, and the lull of gospel

clouding the sweet hiatus
of home and kirk.

Mice in the oat-bin,
honey bees snagging the nets,

and, slowly,
from the stockyards in the town,

the scent of beasts arrives;
the biblical;

rudderless gazes
turned to a farmer's sky.

FOUR QUARTETS

SAINT-NAZAIRE

In history, as in nature, decay is the laboratory of life
Karl Marx

Plane leaves drift through the wynds
around the Catholic church
in Saint-Nazaire,

freeze-dried, silent, wrapping-paper brown,
they gather in the nooks between abandoned
hair salons and shuttered pharmacies,

or swirl around in broken alleyways
till everything is powder – leaves and stalks
and sand-drift, all

in pulverem, except
the rock-cress in the kerbstones and the char-black
ganglia of fallen Judas pods.

I'm walking through the windless innertown,
– breeze-blocks, mongrels, smashed glass, *chantiers* –
walking towards the sky, and the smell of the tide

and reading the names from a map, *rue Lumière,*
impasse de Toutes Aides,
impasse de l'Océan.

Somewhere a bell is ringing,
though whether it comes from the church
or out to sea

49

I cannot tell;
when evening falls, the water bleeds away
towards a rose horizon where the boats

go out to fishing grounds and other
port-towns much like this;
the lights are only brilliant

in the distance, and no matter where we are,
the sea is somewhere else. The constancy
of gulls and harbour seals

belongs to elsewhere, when the moon comes out
and floats above the squalls of Europop,
the neon bars, the hyper Champion,

the kids racing bikes through disused
U-boat hangars, engine roar strafing the walls,
exhaust fumes wreathing the bays

of blue-lit water.
On the bridge to Petit Maroc,
a legend: VAGUER LA NUIT

DANS DES LUMIÈRES NARRATIVES,
an invocation, maybe, or a prayer,
but, really, all there is is what it says:

the wind in my eyes
and the cold making light of the air,
as I wander from lamp to lamp, to the edge of the night,

and stand on the *quai des Marées*
looking out
to the ocean.

As much as anything, I love the pines
that grow along the seafront, making green
the harbour towns and docks
and narrow squares
of dust and shadow, wandering between
the sailors' mission and the Harbour bar;

or, spilled across the duneland in the wind:
sea holly, stonecrop; *panicaut, orpin blanc*:
sand orchid, eel-green and purple: orchis bouc
and orchis bouffon, fat on its silvered stem;

though if I had to choose among them all,
without a doubt, I'd take this common pearl,

this straggled beauty: *immortelle des sables*,
its dry, gold buds
                    vivid against the sand
as nothing is, dug in and everlasting.

The last dusk clings to the walls
of the Hotel de Ville;

at Fleurs du Large,
the Christmas wreaths are out,

fairy lights silver the leaves
of ivy and fir,

the little window
is a memory

of childhood
in the happy-ever-after;

but now they're closing up:
time for the bars

or the absolute quiet of home
when you first turn the key

and everything
that loves an empty room –

dust mote, angel,
hourglass, shadow-play –

settles, or disappears
when you throw the switch

and something,
not quite light, but like

a narrative of light,
a simulacrum, golden, intricate,

resumes, the way a story
is resumed:

table, mirror,
rose bowl, photograph.

On the *rue de Saillé*
a sapling gingko stands

in its own
luminescence;

headlamps
turn through the dark

and find the sea,
white on the water,

moonshine, cobalt blue,
the glowing satsuma

or cherry
of warning lights,

the last mauve of the evening
burning out

along the horizon: nightfall;
endlessness.

To live here is to wait for messengers,
though why the angel takes such differing forms
is always a surprise: cowlicks of snow
on the threshold, the print of a leaf,
tomorrow's shipwreck gusting through the town
as life continues: shopping, memory,
crossing the road in the colourless wake of the dead;

and why does it never happen as it does
in picture books, the categorical,
the diffident stranger poised at the end of the bed,
the wash of the sea at the window, tomcats and birds
about their business on the jewelled lawn?

They quickly forget our names, stillborn and drowned
and second cousins rolled in on the tide,
and everything that lives must fill that space:
the photographs, the stones, the books of salt,
the branches of yarrow, preserved in the leaves of a bible.

It turns out, what we thought of as the soul
is mostly sound;
not song, but like a memory of birds
or running water,
the churn of a paddle, the flicker and dip
of an oar,
narrow boats butting the land
on their quiet tethers,

so death will be a slower, surer fade
than any we imagine;
no mere extinction, like the evening's hush
before the ducks come, dipping to the marsh
in threes and fours, to find the darker ground,
no moment's pause, but absolute decay
where absence is a form
of generation.

Out in the dark, tonight,
our voices drift and sway
like hunting bees,
nothing to those who are going, but the place
they started from:
a given name, a word, a subtle variance
from what endures, the bright unspeakable,
not sky, not earth or flesh,
but finer still,
a call across the lake you half-believe
is nothing, though it happens all the time,
end and beginning,
footfall, leaf-fall, silence.

BY PITTENWEEM

One knows
There is no end to the other world,
                    no matter where it is.
                    Charles Wright

I   HOME

We studied to love the cold,
to make a friend of it, to call it home,

since nothing else
was altogether true,

steeple, or pithead,
bellflower, grandmother's ring;

yet still we were expert
in thaw,

mapping the wetlands,
waiting for crowsfoot to blossom,

fighting the pull of rivers
on April nights,

till all the dreams we had
were dreams of water.

Now, on the fields
and the thrawn trees lining the ditch,

the new sun gathers and runs
like clarified butter,

and, perched on a fence post,
a buzzard extends its wings,

then settles back;
              I'm not a threat to him:
a man without a gun, without a dog,

walking his boundary, measuring,
making good,

I'm not really bound to this place, but
here by choice:

pledged to the first thaw; visible;
out in the open;

accustomed to secrets
and keeping the best of myself

for private use:
a cold blade clenched in my fist

or a length of twine,
my body mapped and measured by the heft

of work that must be done
no matter what.

Springtime again:
              the news all news of flood
and death by drowning,

a levee crumbling away,
a boat going under,

women and children
with faultlines of dread in their faces,

bloated bodies
sprawled on limbs of sand;

and yet, from a distance,
it's hard not to notice the beauty,

the stillness that falls,
the everyday chaos of flotsam,

and, out on a bridge of sandbags,
wed to the rain,

the rescue teams, still working in the dark,
each with his secret, and keeping the best of himself

for hope
          the way the coldest things
give hope:

floodwater, blizzard,
the numb girl pulled from the wreck

still breathing,
in the only home we have:

bone-cold, starlit,
plotted with kill-sites and whispers,

buzzards and starlings
drawn in, then turning away,

spawn in a dew-pond,
stitching the grass with desire.

There was something I heard in the wind,
geese, or the call of a vixen,
or something else, beyond vocabulary;

and sometimes, at night, I feel myself
alone in the dark and looking to see what there is
between the near field and the kitchen door:

the old familiars shifting in the grass
beyond the garden; mute ghosts come from the sea;
the gods that only stones and bulbs recall

rising like smoke and waiting to be found
in the cry of a bird, or the promise of midnight frost;
though nothing will come in a form I could recognise,

no story book figure, no cold face pressed to the glass,
no girl in the attic, weeping, or clutching a doll,
no eerie singing, out along the hedge

some August afternoon.
Tonight, when I stop to imagine, nothing is there,
or only a mist of rain on the left-over pea-sticks,

a glint of light, or something like a cry
that might be nothing;
                                    only the other world
unending, yet lost throughout time

in a circle of light,
a murmur that comes through the wind,
a hand's-breadth, a wingspan,

arriving from nowhere, or conjured up out of the dark
between the near field and the kitchen door,
to sound me out, to comfort me with nothing.

Something that runs to copper
or cornflower blue,

a live creature bounding away
from the glare of my headlamps

and, when the engine stops, a sudden
quiet that waits to be filled

by owls, or cicadas;
though somebody else would say

it's only in the afterlife we get
to talk about such things:

the scent of diesel
misting on our fingers,

a motion in the sky
that never stops,

and how the brimming undergrowth is laced
with boundaries, the softness underfoot

a terminus
              that shifts
and wanders,

              though the end is all it seems:
another colour, not quite red, or mauve,

a trace of cold
more urgent than a kiss,

arriving, like some homespun messenger,
to isolate this waking from the dark.

Pilots and whalers, authorised privateers,
fugitives, botanists, ships' surgeons, makers of maps,
sailing from here, or further along the coast,
to parts unknown;
                            or, half a mile inland,
the old-time celebrants
of seed and weather: tradesmen in their gloves
and aprons; blacksmiths, burnished by the heat
of dark, unending fires; the wandering
haberdasher, cycling round the farms
with cotton twills and satins for a dance;

for all of them, the predicate was home,
if not the world of others, then the world
of all they left unsaid; *that* inwardness:
the house behind the houses in their dreams,
the house of cold, the rooms of fern and bone,
the refuge in a squall, the proof in storms.

All afternoon I waited for the snow,
the horses in the near field staring off
to somewhere memorised: some open plain,
ice in the grass, the grass mapped out in song.
The old potato track, the Lochty line,
is frost and brambles now,
the rattle of old trains sealed in the wood
of fence posts, or that singing in the wires
that mark each neighbour's plot
of whins and stones.

I picture them, shipped in from tenements
and mining towns: mothers and eldest sons,
the casually employed, in hats and scarves,
wet hands numb with the cold
as they follow the tractors,
the life without end of lives that history
finds interchangeable:

                    my mother, say,
in her damp coat and hand-knitted sweater,
leading the way; me, stumbling over the clods
and wishing I was home beside the stove,
clothes hanging up to dry in our steaming kitchen,
the radio playing, those voices from somewhere else
announcing the songs we would hum,
as we counted the hours,
crossing the field, unseeing
and bright with the cold,
everything bleeding away,
to pulp and rain.

All afternoon, I waited for the ghosts
I wanted to find, shapes
shifting in the white
of blizzard,
                    ghosts
not altogether dead, just *cold and gone*;
but when it came, the snow fell urgently
and for the sake of urgency alone,
empty and clear and quick, erasing the road,
erasing the deer-runs and verges, remaking the land
as something unknown and familiar, some holy ground:
the house behind the houses in my dreams,
standing apart, a little cube of lights
and singsong: music; voices from afar;
wind in the phone lines;
the hum of an idling machine.

The worst is to reach the end
and never know:
                    my mother,

dying, say,
pretending the future

existed, when all she had
was an infinite present,

a foreknowledge circling her eyes,
like cold, or soot,

                    a burial
rehearsed between her fingers;

or this old buzzard on the disused
railway line, unravelling his kill,

the winter that might be his last
unfolding around him:

sheep-tracks
and muddled snow,

and the deep sky over his head
unfastened

by the first true white
of stars.

No doubt the earth
forgets us, as we pass

from here to there:
the living and the dead

consanguine, vagrant,
blurring along the walls

like snowdrifts, or some
flicker in the wind,

but this
is neither end

nor resurrection,
only the subtler work

of being:
            birth
in *mutabilitie*,

the black
between the pinion and the snow,

the scattered flesh,
the sweet slur in the dew,

arriving
at a natural conclusion:

logos and water, navelwort,
singing bones,

scavenger warmth
emerging from the cold.

LE CROISIC

Tradition means giving votes to the most obscure of all classes, our ancestors. It is the democracy of the dead. Tradition refuses to submit to that arrogant oligarchy who merely happen to be walking around.
                                        G. K. Chesterton

I SACRED

December; the wind from the point;
nobody here but an old man walking his dog
and a jogger, tuned to the venom
of Eminem.

A flat-boat sits in the harbour, like a lost
sarcophagus: burnished,
abandoned;
a solitary tourist – Japanese, out-of-season –

walks with her trolley-bag to the empty station
to wait for the TGV
while she drinks a soda.
This is the terminus; this is the end of the line:

empty and sacred, a scatter of bells and lights
at the ocean's rim,
and everything else implied: the salt-marsh, the water,
Egyptian ibis, breeding in the dams

and wetlands, hieratic, and far too precise
in their shapes and colours:
an alien species, eternally, wordlessly pledged
to the alien dead.

Nothing is certain here; it's all implication;
in winter, the houses are shuttered
and empty, the antique furniture
still as the wardrobes and chairs

a man sees, when he rises from a dream
of childhood, and his house is strange again,
a borrowed space to shelter from the night,
brimming with insects and shadows, scented with loam,

a simmer of dust in the pipe-work, the guttering candles
and slut's hair of a foreign memory,
smudges of chalk on a mirror, the rust-red or sallow
weathermarks that once were flocks of birds

or ghostly angels, rising through the plaster.
Here, in the off-time, the angels flare from a space
that nobody owns: the moonlight glazing a floor;
the chiming of a clock, still running down

between a locked door
and a flight of stairs
                              — it's all
annunciation,
one way or another,

here, where the fog comes in
from the white Atlantic,
sea-fog, salt-fog,
white on the white of the walls,

voices and wings seeping in
through a broken shutter:

                    all

annunciation,
waiting to be seen

and heard
            – though only in due course:
the householder back from the city in early summer,
unshrouding the tables and desk-lamps, lighting a fire
and finding spots of dust, fogged smears of wax,

smudges of oil on the paintwork,
a hum in his fingers
and something like music
suspended above the rafters.

Nobody sees the angel face to face,
it's mostly induction, a reading of clues and signs
as, after the fact, he remembers the sea as it was
on a specified morning, two or three seasons ago:

how something was there, all along,
in the afternoon light,
the path leading down to the inlet spotted with vetch
and orchids, the flex of the sacred

as faint as a faraway voice
on the shimmering water,
though all that matters now, in this quiet arrival,
is learning to live as a guest in the house he inherits;

         and still the dead are with us,
every day,

coming inland from the point: the meagre dead,
touched with the salt of distance,
                      marked with the blue

of oyster beds
         their faces glimpsed and lost
along the treeline, on another shore;

and surely those others are here,
               the still unborn,
the scent of a world to come
on their eyelids and fingers,

the names they will acquire and wear away
swelling to fit the wind, or burnt by the sun;

though nothing shows: the still of afternoon
continues, while a man in overalls

works on his boat;
         a girl walks to the beach,
pushing a wheelchair: her mother, say,
                 or a friend

of the family, timeworn and empty handed
and leaning
        just a little
           into something

faraway: a frequency,
                    a sky
that no one else can see,
                    another time

unfolding in the light that finds her out
and passes through the needle of her eye:
                              a form

as colourless as birth
or memory.
          Maybe she knows she is going

to meet them again, and maybe she knows their names:
children who drowned in the ocean at Port aux Rocs,

the great-aunt who fell through a dream
of apples and new-washed linen

at Le Paradis.
The man at the edge of the water sets aside

his tools, pulls off
his goggles, and looks to see

how much there is still to do: paint-stains and oil
on his fingers, his sea-coloured eyes

deepened with the years
of ocean light;

he belongs to another time, to the guesswork and craft
of some old clan of seafarers, ready to leave

at a moment's notice, given up for lost
so often, they were traded to the sky

in every song or prayer they left behind
for others to sing or whisper in the dark,

while they sailed on, with the dead
and the unconceived,

betrothed to the space they had glimpsed,
but could never explain

a mile from all they knew: the chapel; the harbour;
the laughter of women; the music of midsummer's eve.

I remember the song they would sing
all the way home from the Woodside, my uncles and cousins,
tarred with the mines and the shipyards, cradled in smoke
and bawling it out, on rain-deadened streets and wynds,
to hear the echo turning in the stones
like déjà vu
            – and still I live in hope to see
the holy ground once more –

What they were looking for, then,
was another beginning,
the black that occasions white, the white in black,
an older soul, exhumed from flesh and bone
to carry on the ancient narrative
of manhood as a song, the savage joy
of bagpipe music, pagan memories,
a host of kinfolk rising from the sea,
a house looming out of the fog
and becoming home.

I think, now, of their disembodied love
and that animal sense I share, in the nerve and the bone
of something urgent, straining from the veins
of holy ground: the hard quotidian;
pit-shafts and docks, harbours and open meadows,
the gap in the hedge, the whisper of running water,
an acre of fog and brambles where something I lost
returned in another form, and was barely remembered.

No permanence is here; no planned Imperium;
this is the holy ground, where nothing happens,
a place we can take for home, when we understand
that it cannot be held, it cannot be taken or given:
egret and cormorant, ibis, the shore birds and waders;
the Japanese tourist; the girl from the waterfront bar;
the clan ghosts and latter-day saints, and the self-appointed
keepers of song and war; the unblinking dead:
everything passes through – but the passing through
is what we think of, now, as sanctuary;

and, sometimes,
nothing will happen:
the world that was ebbing away turns back on itself,
a gust of wind, the sidestreet *bagadou*,
children's voices
gathered in a cypress;
what matters now is not the narrative,
what matters is not the event, but the light-frayed hem
of the moment's annunciation;
what matters is the point where nothing matters:
the gap in the hedge, an acre of fog and brambles
and how the sacred – hard quotidian –
returns to us in songs and superstitions,
an ember that burns in the nerves and the reasoning brain,
a guttering flame, that nothing will ever extinguish –

You see it best from the air:
how salt perpetuates itself, turned from the sea
to whiten the *marais salants*, graded and sieved
and laid in ice-white drifts beneath the sun;

the way you see bonfires or house lights
glimmering in the dark, between the lakes
and cities; marshland dotted here and there
with lanterns; eel boats moving in the dams;

nightfishers coming home with another catch,
the gleam of the deck
and the absolute cold of the nets
deduced, not given.

You see it travelling through: a passenger,
guided from point to point by an unknown hand,
an idling web of memory and salt
turning to glance at the earth, as it slides away

and the slow clouds thicken and gather
beneath the plane.
Below, it's different: the air is wired
with birds and weather; old spills

fester in the ditches; sacred
ibis haunt the marshlands in their
thousands, calling softly back and forth
to wake the shadows of forgotten kings.

Below, on the Place Dinan,
the market is a broken theatre,
tourists go round in circles, looking for gifts
and souvenirs, for little bags of salt

and books of recipes, *galettes* and honeyed *crêpes*
they'll never cook, CDs
of *bagadou*, knitwear and books,
blanched postcards of the salt marsh from the air:

those perfect shapes, those neat, well-managed dams,
those circles of water, dark-blue, like a Celtic
knot, a pattern, conjured from the air
in lines of salt that might be infinite;

or a view of La Côte Sauvage: *le rocher de l'ours*,
the road to Paradise, the Ocearium,
Baie de Cailloux, Plage de Port-Lin,
La Pierre Longue.
Nothing is as it was, even the past
is changing, renewed by a sense
of the past, the *presqu'île* reclaimed
for tradition: *bagad*
and salt marsh, standing stone
and tomb.

The cliff-top houses wait like refugees
from Hopper paintings: boxes filled with light
and silence
        and the people I imagine
walking from room to room, or gazing out
across their wind-stripped gardens, semi-nude
or sitting upright on a sunlit bed,
are people from another place and time,
women in rose-pink dresses, or yellow slips,
old men with faces like birds,
huddled into their bourbon.

This is tradition now: bookplates and posters;
the recognisable; the universal;
scenes from a film I saw in the first year of college
and barely remember: *Vertigo*,
or something by Tati, a cinematographer's light
on the cypress trees and whitewashed
houses; sand
from brochures; sand
and water, where the lovers disappear
in moonlight
        or the dead girl washes up

intact, her beauty
incorruptible.

Nobody meets the messengers face to face;
but sometimes I enter the room
they have just abandoned,
or, crossing the sand, in the quiet of afternoon,
I hear the voice that whispered in my head
a lifetime ago, before the angels turned
to choirboys with wings

and I know what it is we are losing, moment by moment,
in how the names perpetuate the myth
of all they have replaced: windmill and dolmen,
meadow and fishermen's wharf:
a country relearned and forgotten, like the dead
who walk among us, waiting for the day
to light them, on their journey from the known
to the newly strange: to chapel and harbour and hearth,
that slow return from memory to birth
and everything in between: the sea, the sky,
the laughter of women; the music of midsummer mornings.

NY-HELLESUND

*There's not a shadow of a doubt about it, the First Cause
is just unknowable to us, and we'd be sorry if it wasn't.*
                                              D.H. Lawrence

· I   NÅR VI DØDE VÅGNER

A man hears a boat in the sound
and looks up:
his wife is coming home from Kristiansand,
his wife, or a neighbour, or someone he wasn't expecting,
a friend from the city, a niece from the neighbouring island,
a girl he has never seen, in a borrowed boat,
crossing his line of sight, then disappearing;

a man hears an engine crossing the narrow sound
and the beautiful loneliness ends, as the woods shift behind him:
there was something he wanted to fix, there was something he loved,
but no matter how long he sits, or how early he wakes,
the gap between darkness and light has already vanished,
sliding away through the woods,
from island to island,

so all that remains in his room at the top of the house
is the scent on his skin, a scent he mistakes for the spirit,
the smoke from last night's fire, the earth, the grass,
and what the body offers of itself
to any journey, any secret thing
that passes in the dark and flits away:
not self, but history; not self, but place.

A man hears a boat in the sound
and it feels like a gift:
maybe he has lived here all his life
and this is why he knows the commune well,
knows its waters, knows its old stone fences,
knows how, on midsummer nights, when the bonfires are burning,
some pledge in the world recurs, some seamless gift,

so everything comes again, in another form,
not in the shapes we leave
to the tideless water,
not in the phantoms haunting the summer quays
like long-dead forebears, fixed in glass and silver,
holding the pose of a self, through an already
shifting regard, as something away to the left

catches the eye – a shadow, an animal presence –
and whatever they thought they could not do without
is quietly abandoned, while the film
still runs;
           or like a drunkard, on the long walk home,
who finds himself stooping
into a hedge of bees
to catch an injured bird and toss it skyward:

everything comes again, in another form,
much as a mind that is lost
survives through the panic
and comes out, neither fearless nor intact,
but turning back to see a slant of light
and find instruction there: an injured bird,
a fire burning out on the rocks, that blind

– Mor, gi' mig solen –

A freshening rain;
then the sun and the birds
return;

sung and illumined, the island falls into place,
like the raising of the curtain
in a theatre: light
and voices

and the sense that sometimes comes
of having been gone from the world
while the story continued.

It comes of love and hurt;
it comes of fear:
that sudden, immaculate stutter in the heart

as you turn from the path
and everything fades into brightness
– harbour and storm-cloud; memory; companions –

till only the self remains,
an appointed space
where anything might founder;

and sometimes it comes from joy – not
pleasure, or the notion of a life
re-entered, but the panic sinking in

as something happens, like a shifting gear,
or like that moment in a Fifties film
when everyone turns to look, and the stranger is there,

striking a match,
or brushing the snow
from his collar;

and, really, it's not what you meant
by *being alone*;
no matter how it comes, there's always the chill

as something bleeds out in the mind
and you stand abandoned:
wind in the leaves, the new rain spotting your face,

the light on the quay
like a presence that never arrives
and never quite decays

to greenery.
Imagine a god who appears
from nothing, jagged

scrapings in the heart, a ragged nail
tracking the glint of the eye,
or the thrill of the marrow,

and ask yourself
how prayer is possible,
if not to something alien and tidal:

the skitter of a leaf across a window,
a maddened skin
unfolding in the dark;

and whether these prayers arise
from fear, or some extended form
of longing, like the sound the seabirds make

at nightfall,
calling out
along the shore;

whether we pray
to a god, or the weight of an absence,
what matters is the way the story runs

forever,
through the fields of transformation:
terror, a measureless step

on the way to concealment;
concealment, a hidden door
to the currents beyond.

In those stories where one life
shuffles towards another:
child into raven, women to wandering swans,

even the boy in the crawl-space becoming the bear
that finds him by chance
in adventures we scarcely believe,

as no one believes,
to begin with,
in transformation,

the moment we see
as *decisive*, the point of the telling,
is when the changeling peers back at himself

through mist, or rain,
or the haze of a sunlit highway,

and understands that what he leaves behind
is neither the life he possessed, nor his
to abandon,

only a story he learned
as the present unfolded,
setting his hand to the tiller and looking behind him,

or fleshing out the rumours of a death
he'd always known about: the sudden fall;
the gas leak in the night; the epidemic;

some loophole in the memory of water;
the boy who crawled into the jaws
of a sheltering bear

and died, while a foot overhead
his mother was stitching a hem
or setting out dinner.

Or say it went like this: he grew up tall
and married; bought a trawler;
raised his children;

say he grew old
and still never turned to the mirror
at nightfall, when the gloaming on the quay

had settled down
to just that shade of blue
where everything that's lost is rendered

visible,
the god of silt and shipwrecks smeared across
the clouded glass, as if a hand had reached

to wipe his face away
and make him
otherwise:

what if he lived his life as he'd always expected,
no more, no less,
no spectre at the gate, no hidden beauty,

no suspect bowls, set out and then forgotten,
filled with the subtler blue
of an alien nightfall?

surely the changes wait, and will settle in
at the moment he least expects them:
a grand-daughter's wedding; a stop on the way home from market;

surely the shape he fears will arrive to claim him,
beyond all the stories he knows, and the world he possesses,
unbinding his logic, proposing some ancient

IV UN TERRORE DI UBRIACO

after Montale

joy –
which is neither happiness, nor triumph,
and cannot come from anything
but passing through the white of dissolution;

perhaps, on a day like this, the morning air
like cut-glass, I will turn around to see
the miracle:

the nothing at my shoulder, utter void
caught in the sudden twist
of a drunkard's terror;

perhaps, like the beginning of a film,
the world will come again: houses and trees
and nuzzling hills, returning one by one
for the grand illusion;

though by then it will be too late
as I hurry on,
among those who have never looked back,
with my given secret;

or shot rhubarb clogging the ditch,
harbouring blackness, shaping the pull of the water;
goldfinches tracking the verge as a car runs on
and, almost asleep at the wheel, the driver
slides into beauty:
seed drift and dipping flight, and the shift of the charm
as it gathers and turns, then, all of a sudden,
is gone, while he wakes to the cats' eyes'
calibrated

judder;
      wakes,

though not to what he knows:
the daylight altered, nothing at the windscreen,
lit trees lining the road
at the edge of the storm.

Sometimes the only tool we have
is panic,
not what was wanted, perhaps, but something to work with,
a shape at the edge of vision, a spill in the gut,
a colour we cannot name, though it seems familiar

I'll sing you five, O
Green grow the rushes, O
What are your five, O?
Five for the symbols at your door,
Four for the Gospel makers,
Three, three, the rivals,
Two, two, the lily-white boys,
Dressed up all in green, O
One is one and all alone
And evermore shall be so

and there it is once more, the freshening rain,
better than all he has lost, and beyond his keeping:

In the dreams I remember
of childhood,

we cross to the far side of town
to begin among strangers,

shy of asking favours from the folk
we know, and thinking these others

rich, for their pot-pourri
and antimacassars,

though what I like best is going, as someone else,
in the flow of the wind,

to stand, in my pirate shirt, at a foreign door
and catch the scent of someone else's house,

coffee and gelatine, rose petals, sickness, books,
the trace of powder on a printed shawl

left draped across a chair, that lampshade smell
of winter evenings, everything they took

for granted: glacé
cherries, candlewax,

the slow fade of themselves
grown old, or too long paired

with childhood sweethearts: disappointments shared
so quietly, they came, each Halloween,

to seem a little more
like blessings, when they lingered at the door

to bear us witness:
damp eyes peering out

to find us in the dark, like long-lost friends
– a pirate child, a chimney sweep, a king –

come from the first chill of winter
and dusted with nothing.

The corn is full of skylarks;
the last of the daylight
simmers above the wood
where chiffchaff and warblers
parley from shade to shade,
becoming the air
in a song that exists for nothing.

Everything maps its world
and what world there is
is the current sum
of all our navigation:
networks of panic and longing,
road maps in gorse,
the river at twilight
vanishing into the sway
of cattle and bees;

and nothing is ever as true as the darkness of home:
the porch-lights we know by name, the pea-fields and crossroads;
deer-run and spawn-pool, birdwalk and dead man's curve,
the wide night running away
to campsites and dairies,
or junior hockey teams, in red and blue,
rehearsing the perfect game
in a circle of rainfall.
This is a map of forever, all pitfalls and tremors,
a glister of stars in the distance, a body of fire,
eels on a towpath, charting the grass between rivers,
the thinning beauty of the long way home
and, somewhere in the dream beyond this dream,
the house behind the houses I remember,
frog-house, star-house, house of silk and tuber,

the tribes of visitants who come and go,
touched with the green of the woods, or the green of water:
shapes I have seen in glimpses, through panic and joy:
palms and glances sliding through the headlamps,
stickle-bones, whiter than chalk, in the faultlines of weather

and somewhere in the dream behind this dream
an acre or so of pine and sycamore;
where people go out in the gloaming,
for no good reason,
trading secrets, trading hurt and longing,
or, solitary, raking out a stash
of dirty pictures: dreams of flesh and steel
and headstrong women, waiting to be mastered

but home is where everything happens: panic and joy,
the meeting with the god, that stink of goat;
hairless angels stepping from the rain;
here, in a strip of woodland, driving north,
through everything I've seen and heard before

though nothing I see is ever seen enough,
nothing is heard for certain, even the rain
as it falls through the glamour
of streetlamps and dormer windows
a mile from my destination: everything seen
and heard, everything known
resembles the self, or rather, that sense of a self
that might have been, at one remove from here,
perfect, like the rumoured fall of snow
that no one ever witnessed, though they say
it happened, just a block or two away,
and sensible people, people much like ourselves,

abandoned what they were doing and ran outside
in their shirt sleeves, drawn by instinct to the place
where bodies formed, great waves of sound and light
becoming fingers, eyelids, shoulders, hair.

ACKNOWLEDGEMENTS

Acknowledgements are due to the *London Review of Books*, *Paris Review*, *Poetry Review* and *The Times Literary Supplement*.

I wish to thank the Scottish Arts Council, for financial assistance during the writing of this book. I would also like to acknowledge the support of all at La Maison des Ecrivains Etrangers et Traducteurs, especially Patrick Deville, Elisabeth Foucault and Jean Rolin.

'Quartet: Saint Nazaire' was commissioned by the Bath Festival; 'Quartet: Le Croisic' was commissioned by La Maison des Ecrivains Etrangers et Traducteurs; to both organisations, my thanks.